MW00905508

Co-collaborator, my wife Sue Mason
Illustrated by Michael S. Handorf.
Formatting and Editing by Leia Shouey
Printed by Amazon, in the United States of America.

First printing edition 2023.
n.nelsonqb@gmail.com

The Steps to Pickleball Recovery

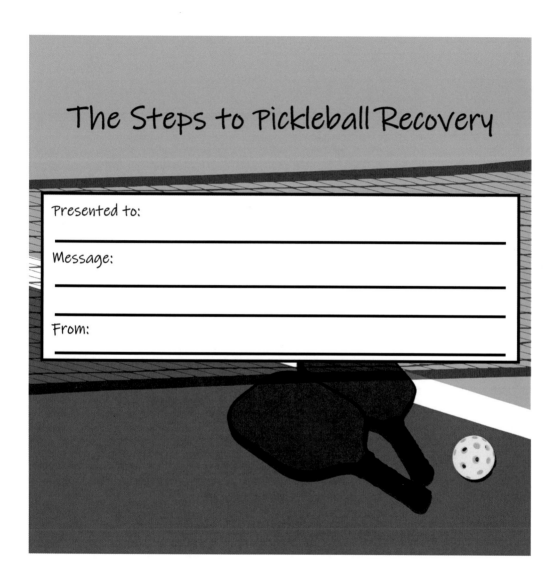

Presented to:
_____

Message:
_____

_____

From:
_____

The Steps to Pickleball Recovery
Forward

What is this force that drives me on, its nature I don't know.

From park to park and court to court, and onward I must go!

Why must I play everyday morning, noon, and night,

What is this thing I cannot shake, that grips me with a fright?

It started off so innocent, a purchase just to see.

I'll buy a paddle and check it out, "It's probably not for me".

A simple little past pastime that started off so nice

Has taken over my life, and now become my vice!

I commit myself to these steps

To release from the power that pulls me in,

That haunts my mind, that fills my waking hours.

I will not be drawn into the pull of the pickleball

I will not pay monthly dues, to play inside at all

I will not stand in the sun and run and sweat and "dink"

My mind is strong, my will is hard, my armor has no chink.

The Steps to Pickleball Recovery

Step 1-Helpless

I admit I have succumb, to the Pickleball phenomenon

Overwhelmed I lack the power to pull myself away,

I cannot bear to manage these decisions every day!

Where to go, and who to play...oh to be a psychic,

The pleasure and the pain it brings, I can't believe I like it!

I rush off to the courts, I play, and I play, I try so hard to improve my game

Must get better everyday, should I change my paddle?

Should I change my ball, should I take more lessons or have I hit the wall?

I release this thing I cannot control, a force that keeps me dinking.

I admit and bear the pains, whatever was I thinking!

The Steps to Pickleball Recovery
Step 2-Admit Mistakes

I'm sorry for the trash talk, about the other team
I'm sorry for the gloating, and acting really mean

I'm sorry for the smashes, that caused my friends to bruise
I'm sorry for my ugly thoughts when you made me lose

I'm sorry for the line calls, that I said were out
I'm sorry for the swear words, I really shouldn't shout
I'm sorry when I cheated, and there really was no doubt
I'm sorry for the cracked balls that I said were fine

I'm sorry you had to listen to all the times I whined
I'm sorry for a lot of things...I have a whole lot more

But I'm really sorry I played as a 3,
When I really was a 4!

The Steps to Pickleball Recovery
Step 3- Help me

I believe there is a power, greater than my own,
Who knows I crave to play on every court I am shown.

Who understands my weakness and sees me for my self.
Who gives me strength to stop and leave that paddle on the shelf.

Who understands this malady, this ailment, this affliction.
Who understands the depths of this powerful addiction!

Who knows how hard I've tried to keep the pickleball at bay,
This thing that calls my name out, each and every day.

My desire to play in every game, I attribute to my vanity.
I know I'll be restored, and I will regain my sanity.

Help me for you understand, this game is just like crack,
The craving such a burden, heavy on my back
But this monkey's not a large thing, it's really very small,
It's plastic and it's full of holes, it's called a pickleball!

The Steps to Pickleball Recovery
Step 4- Remove the Flaws

Please remove the defects from my character concerning

All the changes in my essence, that have slowly been emerging.

Looking back to what this was, and when I felt the call,

I wish that I had never known or heard of pickleball!

Developed on a weekend, amusement for a child,

Then turned into obsession, a game that has gone wild.

A simple game consisting of a paddle and a ball,

You hit back and forth across the net, in an area rather small.

Something that you would enjoy on a sunny afternoon,

Not meant to cause frustration, is making me a loon!

The Steps to Pickleball Recovery
Step 5- Stop the Excess!

My 1st paddle came from Goodwill, the next one from the store.

Number 3 was for my birthday, for Christmas number 4,

5 seemed to be too many, then later not enough,

7 paddles later, now I've got a lot of stuff!

Shirts and shoes, balls, and cups, and knickknacks all round,

I bought a bigger sports bag, that now weighs 30 pounds.

Then I bought a better sports bag, that mentions pickleball,

I thought it made me cooler, but that was not the case at all.

Now there's a pickleball closet, that I've been hiding for a while

But I'm seeking will and knowledge and admitting my denial.

The Steps to Pickleball Recovery
Step 6- Look Inside

I commit I will look within, and make a moral fearless quest,

To determine why pickleball makes me act possessed?

Why is it that I stand in line, in the heat and cold

waiting for another game, it never does get old.

Why do I try and justify, a game that's such a chore,

Before I finish one game, I'm thinking, I should play five more?

I think of so much pickleball, I think that I'm a freak,

I threw my remote across the room, while serving in my sleep!

I will inventory all my thoughts, and carefully reflect,

Is this action normal or is there serious disconnect?

The Steps to Pickleball Recovery
Step 7- Imperfections

My shortcomings weren't an issue, not even worth a mention,
But now because of pickleball, they require some intervention!

Unacceptable behaviors that grew out of this quest,
This flaw within my nature, requires I take a rest.

Challenge play in the mornings, round robins in the afternoon
I've spent too much time away, I've got to change that soon.

My spouse thinks I am cheating, I'm getting a lot of questions,
I guess I shouldn't ask, my partners for suggestions?

I'm searching for some answers, I want to be OK…
Just don't ask that question, "Pickleball today?"

The Steps to Pickleball Recovery
Step 8- Remorseful

I admit to myself and everyone I know,
That I have wronged, in my effort to make my rating grow.

I started off as a 2, then kept working for a 4
The time and the money spent, I'd rather just ignore.

Forgive me for the stress was great, the practice and the tension.
It made me do some ugly things, I'd rather just not mention!

I made up some appointments and said things that weren't true,
Just to get to the courts and play another game or two.

At work they think I'm busy, but I'm searching on the net
Searching for some Pickleball…another big regret!

These regretful acts committed in my course to seek perfection
I attribute to my passion, and the use of poor discretion.

The Steps to Pickleball Recovery
Step 9- Release Me

To God I give this burden, I place it in his care.

I know that he will help me, and keep me from despair.

Don't let me think of playing, keep pickleball from my mind,

Give me horseshoes, golf or cricket, a sport of any other kind.

I went to church to focus. I was looking for support...

They had moved all the chairs away, the church was center court!

So, I decided on some yoga, to center up my core,

I couldn't hear my chanting, there was pickleball next door.

Then I went to seek some therapy, I was really out of sorts,

I drove down to the office; they had all turned into courts.

Running from pickleball, has turned into a horror,

It's like trying to quit drinking, with a bar on every corner!

The Steps to Pickleball Recovery
Step 10- Atonement

To all my fellow workers, forgive me for the years
Of pickleball conversation, that bored you all to tears.

Who uses what? Who's out on top? What paddle is the best?
I'm recovering from pickleball, I'm sorry I'm so stressed!

Please let me back in the normal group, I swear this is the end,
Can't we just start over and we'll all be friends again?

I'll only speak of current things, food and maybe news,
I'll take down all my posters, and the paddles I will lose.

I won't be leaving early, for lessons or for games,
No more extended lunches or excuses that are lame!

The Steps to Pickleball Recovery
Step 11- Realization

To the family who shared the pain of my rocky course,
I want to tell you all, that I'm feeling deep remorse.

For the many times I faltered, I'm grateful that you stayed.
I left you all alone, while I went off and I played.

I know I went overboard and purchased lots of items,
Cups, shoes, shirts and hoodies, I'm ashamed I had to hide them.

I'm sorry that I spent our cash and caused so much frustration,
I promise no more tournaments, and no more lost vacations,

Yes, I joined into the madness, but this is where it ends,
It's time to leave pickleball alone and let the hurting end.

The Steps to Pickleball Recovery
Step 12- Help Those Who Fall

I must meditate and concentrate on what it means to me,
To walk away and truly say, that I am really free.

Keep focused on my goal and the power not to fall,
Back into the habit, of playing pickleball.

Don't let me fall back in again, to suffer from regression,
I'm keeping my resistance strong through continuous confession.

It's been tough, I've had enough, I'm picking-up the pieces.
I almost caved, but then was saved, as my urging now decreases!

Each and every one of us, must prop-up those that fall,
You'll know them by the pattern, of nonstop pickleball!!!

The Steps to Pickleball Recovery
So this is the end…

This isn't something local, an illness we should hide.
This problem reaches millions, afflicting world-wide!

It doesn't know your race, your religion or your sex,
It doesn't care who you are or the cause of its effects.

We can only save so many through our caring and our teaching.
It cannot be subdued when the growth is so far reaching.

Beware the early symptoms, they come upon you quick,
A few games here and there & before you know it, you are sick!

Giving up the life you knew and forsaking everyone and all,
You're drawn into this sickness, this thing called Pickleball!

The Steps to Pickleball Recovery
Now I'll Move on...

Now I've recovered and shunned pickleball,

I will travel the states and reject it all...

I won't wake up each day and just wait to play

I'm trying new things, I'm going away!

I'm going to travel and try a new life,

One without courts and one without strife

I want to forget and I want to expand,

And I want to do it, without a paddle in hand.

The Steps to Pickleball Recovery
Oregon

I went to Oregon to commune with the trees

I went to a clearing and got down on my knees

I was meditating deeply when a bear came along

He picked up my pack and then he was gone!

I walked for 8 hours because the bear had my keys,

That is the last time that I will get down on my knees,

Give me a break, Oregon and trees!

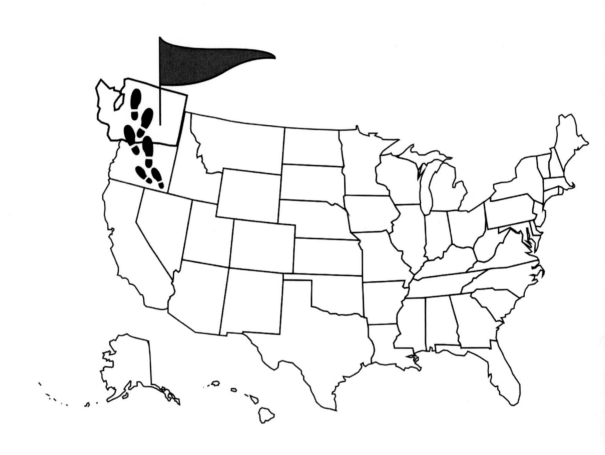

The Steps to Pickleball Recovery
Seattle

I went to Seattle where famous coffee was born
The coffee shop people, were really forlorn,

So, I stood at the ocean and I made a wish.
I went to the market where they threw me a fish

I took an underground tour where I saw a rat
I went to a café that had too many cats
I got up for a napkin and two cats came up
One licked my coffee, the other his butt

I almost got mugged when I went downtown,
I think I'll move on, to more fertile ground!

The Steps to Pickleball Recovery
Am I there yet?

Well, I've been to two states

And I can say, overall...

That I still have the urge, to play pickleball!

I've traveled a lot and I'm starting to think,

Maybe I should go back to the DINK!

But I'm resisting that urge and as I said once before,

Forget pickleball,

I will travel some more...

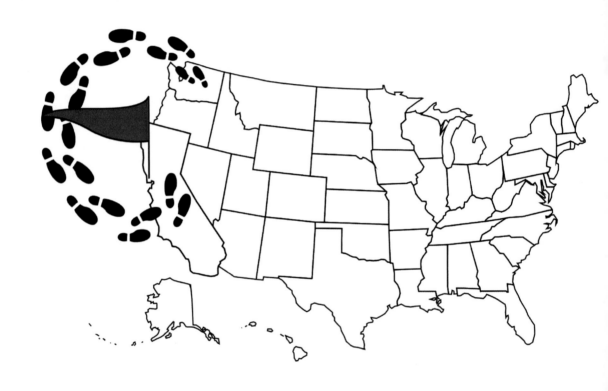

The Steps to Pickleball Recovery
San Francisco

I went to San Francisco, the beautiful bay

A lot of people warned me, just stay away!

I said away from the Bridge, the Wharf and the shore,

What a wonderful place, who could ask for more?

I went to the Bridge, where I got hit by a car

I went out on a boat, and puked in a jar

I went to the shore, and stepped on some glass

You can keep San Francisco

I think I will pass!

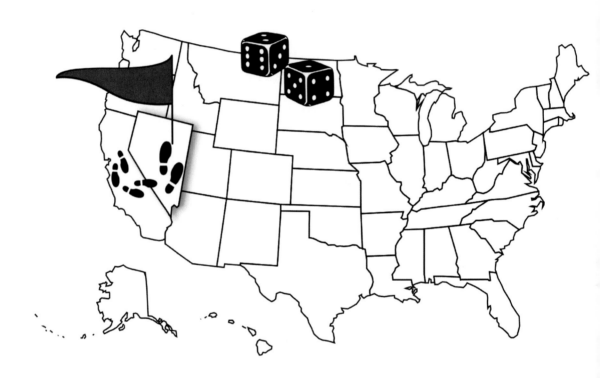

The Steps to Pickleball Recovery
Nevada

I went to Nevada, the Silver State;
The gambling, the night life, I heard it was great

Some said you must see the burning man show
It's out in the dessert, you really must go.

Oh! The things that I saw
The nudity, oh my!

I partied so hard and gave strange things a try,
Forget you Nevada, I'll never be back!

I now have a tattoo of a witch and cat.

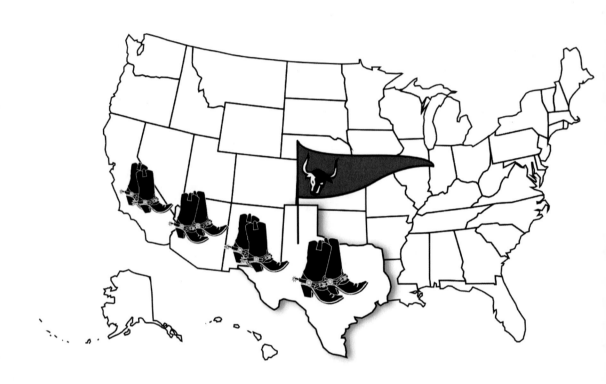

The Steps to Pickleball Recovery
Texas

I traveled over to Texas, the old Lone Star State
I went to see the Alamo, but they closed the gate

So, I went into a cowboy bar and jumped up on a stool.
No one wanted to dance with me,
so I said I'll show them that I'm cool.

I got on that mechanical bull and hollered "turn it on Jack,"
It spun around once or twice and I quickly heard a crack!

I got off bending over and walking really slow,
I couldn't dance or put on my pants for three days in a row

So I guess I'm not a cowboy, or even very tough
Moving on from Texas, they play a little rough

The Steps to Pickleball Recovery
Florida

I decided I needed to go far away
So I went down to Florida for a few days.

Of all the places to travel in all,
I went to the Mecca of Pickleball!

Here I am trying to heal and to mend
when I walked straight into the lions den.

Never have I seen so much pickleball
They said numbers were growing and that wasn't all,
They said they currently had over one thousand courts,
I started to faint and was a bit out of sorts!

I thought if this many people are playing the game,
Maybe I'll go back and I'll do the same?

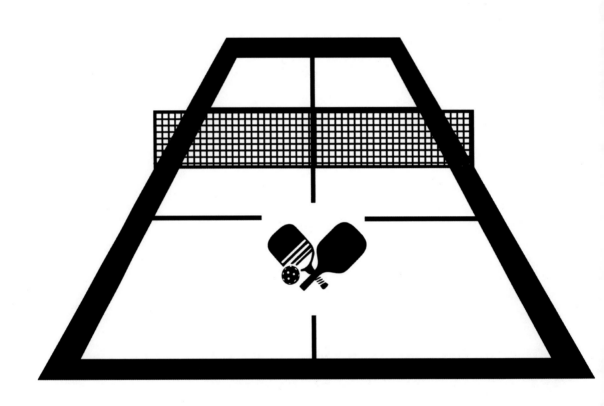

The Steps to Pickleball Recovery
I'm Back...

You know I traveled the States, I gave it a try
I saw many things, under our big sky

I opened my mind to the things that I found
And tried to relate to those all around

I realize now that I wasn't lost,
All good things, do come with a cost

I know without Pickleball I'm not complete,
I need me some Pickleball and I need to compete!

So, I'm going back to the thing that I love
The dinking, the smashing, and wearing a glove
I know it's addicting and it takes all my time

But I love it, I live it and I know that it's mine!

Made in the USA
Las Vegas, NV
24 November 2023

81453108R00031